T0146571

Pieces of Me

Poems, prayers and psalms

Kerisha Leone

WESTBOW
PRESS®
A DIVISION OF THOMAS NELSON
& ZONDERVAN

Scripture quotations are from The Holy Bible, English Standard Version® (ESV®), copyright © 2001 by Crossway, a publishing ministry of Good News Publishers. Used by permission. All rights reserved.

Taken from THE JESUS BOOK - The Bible in Worldwide English © 1969, 1971, 1996, 1998 by SOON Educational Publications, Willington, Derby, DE65 6BN, England

WestBow Press books may be ordered through booksellers or by contacting:

WestBow Press
A Division of Thomas Nelson & Zondervan
1663 Liberty Drive
Bloomington, IN 47403
www.westbowpress.com
1 (866) 928-1240

Because of the dynamic nature of the Internet, any web addresses or links contained in this book may have changed since publication and may no longer be valid. The views expressed in this work are solely those of the author and do not necessarily reflect the views of the publisher, and the publisher hereby disclaims any responsibility for them.

Any people depicted in stock imagery provided by Thinkstock are models, and such images are being used for illustrative purposes only. Certain stock imagery © Thinkstock.

ISBN: 978-1-5127-3869-8 (sc)
ISBN: 978-1-5127-3870-4 (hc)
ISBN: 978-1-5127-3868-1 (e)

Library of Congress Control Number: 2016906166

Print information available on the last page.

WestBow Press rev. date: 05/17/2016

'Pieces of Me' is dedicated to YHWH
the author and finisher of my faith.
To my mum, the lioness and my number one
cheerleader, I love you with all my heart.
This book is to inspire those who have
lived through or are in dark places
right now. I just want to say the storm
will pass...trust and believe.

This book contains poems, prayers, songs and just my thoughts. It's sort of a diary of an average girl from London who likes to ponder about God and life from time to time.

"Yahweh came down in the cloud and spoke to him, and took of the Spirit that was on him and put it on the seventy elders. When the Spirit rested on them, they prophesied, but they did so no more." (Numbers 11:25)

When Moses was tired God gave
seventy elders part of
Moses' spirit. I believe that
part of your spirit is left
with people through the words that we speak. I
would love to inspire/influence/
encourage seventy people,
but even if I inspire one that
is still an achievement
which is what this book aims to
do. I aim to inspire you to
come out of dark places and
discover the treasure
within you when you do. I was
inspired to write this
book while going through a
dark place. Everybody

will go through something in
life that sets them back
or causes you to reevaluate life. We should be
grateful for these times because
likened to the grape
or the olive they are crushed in order to be
transformed into something greater.

Contents

Food for Thought

It is good to have a positive mind
and be of good courage in times of
adversity. Otherwise you feel
yourself going into a downward
spiral of darkness.
It is good to kill the flesh and put on
humility, always esteeming others
before yourself. It is hard to do that I'm
not even going to lie, just like it is
hard to love. To balance having humility but not
having low self esteem is an art. I pray lord that
you will give me the strength from day to day to
do this. Sometimes I just want to run away and
hibernate but we are the light
of the world and the
salt of the earth. We are not put here to be
hidden away, but that others may praise God
because of us. I have made some silly mistakes
Father because I have been walking
by sight. I have been pondering in my
mind what it means to be truly like your
son and boy is it a heavy cross to

bear. To die to self is extremely painful while you are still living. To be corrected is extremely painful and so is being wrong and having to make things right. To realize that I actually know nothing in the grand scheme of things and to trust you even when I can't trace you is so hard. I'm gonna try my best to fight the good fight of faith and to be a good soldier of Jesus Christ.

My All

My love, my Lord,
My peace, my joy,
My provider, my friend,
My beginning and end,
My morning, my guide
In whom I shall abide
My hope, my shield,
My spirit I yield
My king, my light,
My strength, my might,
my food, my mother
My father, my brother,
The key and the door,
The shepherd to the sheep,
The breath of my life,
My faith when it's weak,
My star that burns brightly by night and day,
My truth, my gate, my keeper, my way
The fire in the hearts who desire to follow,
The fullness in my spirit when it's hollow,
My comforter, protector, creator and helper,

Through the storms of my life
you have been my shelter.
Thank you, Jesus.

Trust Him

Trust in Yahweh with all your heart and
don't lean on your own understanding...
-Proverbs 3:5

I trust Yahweh because I know He loves me
I trust Yahweh because He has
revealed that He has
chosen me
I trust Yahweh because I no longer have fear in
His presence
I trust Yahweh because He is
my confidence and my
strength
I trust Yahweh with my deepest
secrets that He knows
even before I confess them
I trust Yahweh because He
comforts me when I'm lonely
I trust Yahweh because everything I am today is
because of Him

Why do you trust and believe in Him?

Don't Worry

Only you, my Lord, can change my situation,
With no boundaries and no limitations,
No hindrance and no hesitation,
For you, my Lord, nothing is too hard

Don't worry about a thing
You're never alone
Don't worry about tomorrow
It will take care of its own
Be of good courage; he strengthens the broken
hearted
Don't let doubt put you out, finish
the race you started.

Only God can see what you try to hide;
Hurts that haunt you and tears you up
inside, you won't tell anyone or swallow your
pride, but God is always by your side.

When walls and obstacles are in your way,
Don't be scared to lift your voice to pray

He listens to every word and will
answer according to his
will.

Beloved

My beloved is mine, and I am his
Intoxicated in each other's
love, we see no other.
This is our world of beauty,
bliss, and blessed love.
You are always thinking of me,
caring for me in ways that only my soul
understands.
You understand me, and I understand you
in a language that goes beyond words.
Your love is amazing and life changing.
As it overflows to our children,
your heart is big and soft.
Your warrior-like exterior encases a precious
heart that you have entrusted to me. I am
blessed to be the keeper of your heart,
the queen to the kingdom of your heart.
You also hold the keys to my heart.
You have cultivated me and allowed me to grow
like the sunshine, you nourish
me. You protect me like a
delicate flower.

Let us be fed from each other's wellsprings, the fresh water that gives life. I am in you and you are in me, because we are one. This is what is true love, you lay down your life for me. I will submit and revere you always. So let it be done on earth as it is in heaven.

Xxxxxxx

Live Right

Instead of wrong, you must do right
Don't walk in darkness but in the light
Stay close to God and you will see
In every sin he'll set you free.
The moment you say yes to
him your spirit is made
clean,
No need to be scared of evil, you're on the
winning team.
Read the word daily, and prayer is the key,
You'll become a threat to evil and the Devil will
flee,
So if you feel you're falling,
or sinking in the sand
Just remember God upholds you in his mighty
hand.

Under Construction

When I look back on the things
you have done, it's
amazing to see the good works you've begun,
in me. I have the assurance
that you will complete
what you've started.
I will follow you whole-heartedly,
as your spirit inspires
me to think upon you
In all that I say and all that I do
I delight in your works and
the things I have seen
Through the turbulent storm and
the very calm stream
In the lives of those who believe
and have not seen
You become real to us through
your Word and in dreams.
Inspire us to become wise in the
eyes of those who don't perceive
the lies that the world portrays.
Give us the power to influence
them to gain everlasting days.

The Man Who Walked on Water

This song goes out to the man
who walked on water.
When the storm breaks out the
wind and seas obey his order,
Order my steps; lead me with your hand,
Teach me how to understand,
Keep me under the shadow of your wings,
So that I may not seek after empty
things.

Humility

Don't be quick to judge today,
For you could fall tomorrow.
The sins you've sown today
Could reap a harvest of sorrow.
Confess your sin to God so
that he may blot it out,
So you can praise his name and
know what love's about.
Turn away from wickedness
and the iniquity you do,
And repent so that the times of
refreshing may come upon you.

Blinded by Love?

Didn't wanna see it coz I was blind
Didn't wanna hear it coz I was proud
When I could hear the spirit saying
out loud, to leave him alone.
Kept on telling myself it would be all right.
Love is blind, but now I see. I never thought
it would happen to me, but it did.
Have you ever blinded yourself
to what you think is love?
How many of us have done something
foolish in the name of love?
Yet we fall for it every time
Love is a powerful thing. Just wish it was pure.
It's like: why can't it just be reciprocated?
People often get hurt because the love
in a relationship is imbalanced.
Someone always loves the other person more
Can't we compete for who can out
love each other rather than who looks
the best or has the best sex?
But the more I talk about it, I can feel in my
bones, that he is near - my husband that is LOL.

He is closer than ever as I approach each day
Gentle, kind, and loving. Good-
looking and a great physique, taller
than me so I can wear heels
(Okay, I'm going off on a tangent
now. How did we get
here?) See how the mind can spiral
out of control? Is that what happens
when we get lost in love?

The Company You Keep Is So Important

Don't waste your time on things that are simple.
Make the most of opportunities
because the days are evil.
Don't try to fit in with people;
Those who have no dream.
Take a step back to observe the scene.
Know where you are going and have a plan.
The Lord orders the steps of man,
Coz ordinary just won't do.
Being unique is not being someone
else, but being you.

Memories

Memories from the corners of mind
I think about you, every time I
hear the song we like
Just the other day, I saw someone
who looked like you
Gets so frustrating. Can't seem
to keep my mind off
you.
I know that I've got to let go,
Move on, be strong,
But it's easier said than done.
Funny how you're the only one who
has this effect on my mind.
You planted so many emotional land mines,
Songs, smells, places, and words you said,
Always pop up in each waking
moment to remind me of you.
Memories from the corners of my mind.
I try to keep my mind off you,
But you return there every time

May even smell someone wearing
the cologne you used to wear
This is getting so bad, but I don't
think you even care.

No Rewinds

Many a times I ask God why I
met you, because I regret
that I did.
I was so stupid to think that I could change you,
Got shot by cupid far too soon,
If I didn't have God, I could have
lost my mind long ago.
All the time, I thank God for peace of mind.
Keeps me moving forward, coz
there's no rewinds in life.
Never would have taken the chance on you,
If I knew you would change,
Wouldn't have given you a second glance,
If your personality wouldn't rearrange
I need not worry because what
God has for me is mine,
Only he can open the necessary doors for
me, You may not think things are working,
Circumstances you may see won't be forever.

So have joy and be happy in the now,
Things can only get better, Just believe
that it's true. People change all the time
But The Lord never fails you.

Speak Those Things...

Finally you are here.
The man I've been waiting for all my life.
Where have you been hiding? I'm so happy
because you were definitely worth the wait.
If I didn't have to sift through the
rubbish, I would have missed you and
probably wouldn't appreciate you.
It's amazing how you love me, nurture and take
care of me. I could not have even imagined that
your love could be this good. You treat me like a
Queen and you are the King I've been waiting
for my whole life. Strong, fun, intellectual and
gentle. Smooth and warrior-like, all at the
same time. The love we share is romantic
but true. I feel safe when I'm with you. I feel
protected and there is nothing you won't give
to me. Yet you are wise and focused on your

goals. You are action oriented and inspire me to be creative. You support my dreams and calm my fears by encouraging me. This love is true and good and pure and God given. Thank you Father. Xxxx

Broken Hearted

"Yahweh is near to those who
have a broken heart..."
-Psalms 34:18

Thank you for breaking my heart
into a million pieces.
For walking out of my life and
making me feel so rejected.
Now if that didn't happen, I would never have
experienced what it's like to be treated so good.
To be treated like a lady and to be valued and
appreciated. Not only am I
appreciated but I appreciate
him. I'm so glad I didn't end up
with you because I'm so
happy. Praise The Lord for light
afflictions because I have
completely healed from that era
of my life. Thank God for
a speedy recovery. Ladies and
gentlemen I once heard a

preacher say "If people walk out
of your life, let them walk,
if they were meant to stay, they
couldn't leave and if they
were meant to leave they couldn't
stay". Just be grateful
when God closes the door on
that toxic relationship,
because there is better...trust and believe.

Emotions

Feelings of anger, feelings of rage.
Appearing upon this side of the page.
My life is a book with chapters of fears,
Chapters of love, chapters of tears.
Different characters are introduced each time
Each have a paragraph or maybe a line.
Some pass through, and some stay till the end.
Understanding me can be hard to
comprehend, But don't judge me by
the cover, read between the lines.
You'll find the secrets that are left behind
Once the page is turned you
can't turn them back.
Just keeping turning until you
reach the hard back.
How many pages till then I don't know.
How many chapters till then I don't know.
But what I do know is some pages are missing.
Pages of instruction and listening

Direction and guidance
Happiness and finance.
Maybe it's in the next chapter
or even the next two
But one things for sure and true,
No matter what happens the author never fails.
This is real life and not fairy tails
He's in control from page one, until the story
dun! We should all have love, wisdom and good
advice, I'm a book of life bought with a price.

The Inner Conflict

My mind is full of faith and my
body full of selfishness.
Father purge me from my inner sin of bad
mind. Keep my thoughts pure and far from
evil. Purge me from unrighteousness and
create in me a clean heart daily. Allow me to
sow good seed and to reap good fruit in due
season. Allow me to become a better person
from the wretched person that I am. Free me
Lord and hear my cry. All I need is a day in
your presence to learn the meaning of love.
One moment is all it takes for me to see a
clear path of wisdom and understanding. Lord
you look at the heart and not the outward
appearance, which means you, cannot be
emotionally blackmailed or manipulated. So
allow me Lord to come correct in your sight,
may my thoughts and deeds be pleasing to you.

Spiritual Warfare

The enemy try's to play me with his bag of tricks
Touch this; God will crush you with his iron fist.
Guarantee he won't miss
Forget your hit list, no matter
what God is in the midst.
Not perfect but I won't quit
Yeah I do wrong God knows it
You might sway the world, but God owns it.
And I won't get bun in the fire, you're a liar, I
won't get bun in the fire, I'm soaring higher.
To higher heights, try to take this life?
Not now, no way, no how, not ever it's over
Don't need a four leaf clover
I got Jehovah,
I'm more than a soldier
More than a warrior, a conqueror
Continuing with the race.
So you can keep up the chase
And I may make mistakes,
But I won't stop till I seek his face
And I can't stop till I find my place,
and I don't care how long it takes
I'd rather do it now before it's too late.

I'm Not Done With You Yet!

I'm not done with you yet!
You've still got so much to do and see.
Hold on to your vision because
it was given from me.
I'm not done with you yet!
Grab your dream and run with it
Ensure that you fulfill it and
don't hide your promises.
Believe in what you expect,
I'm not done with you yet!
It's not by my strength that I am who
I am today. It's not by my power
that I'll be who I'm gonna be
But it's by your Spirit that lives in me that gives
me hope and direction.
A total connection to you, Oh Lord.
I can think of no greater place
than in your presence.

A God forsaken place is a
fearful and terrible place.
I thank you Lord that no matter what, through
your Son we can come boldly to your throne.

The Greatest Love

Your love is everlasting.
Your love is unchanging.
Your love is incredible
Your love is so amazing.
The way you love me is above all things
Nothing can separate me from this
The greatest thing is that I don't deserve it,
And even so you allow me to grow.
How much you love me, no one even knows.
There is no higher price for my life than
the blood of Christ, Who left the throne
in order to save my life. In order to give
me power, authority and control.
To see myself for who I am and make me whole.

The One

Confidently he walks over to me, the
man of my dreams or so it seems.
Coffee-brown skin, could it be him?
The one that I've been searching for.
Looking deep within as we
converse on our first date.
Heads turn as we laugh for hours on end.
Not only is he a lover but a beautiful friend.
He is strong not just physically but emotionally,
Gifted and brought up well. He is a teacher
of life and we learn from each other.
He is gentle and kind and he
knows he's found a dime,
He speaks with clarity and authority,
a well-rounded person.
Not perfect but willing to learn from
life lessons. Mature in his mind and
character, respectful to his mother.
I'm so happy that I can see no other.
Embraced in each other's love,
I think you were sent from heaven above.

Fulfilled

I believe that what your word says is true
I shall trust in you and not be sad or blue.
Your mercy is everlasting and
you are always forgiving
I will witness your goodness in
the land of the living.
Whatever the heart is full of the mouth speaks
My heart is full of joy and my happiness leaks.
It is contagious and by their
fruits you shall know them
Embrace like minded people and show them.
Step into your destiny and lead by example
Treasure your water supply
because you have ample.
Unlock your treasure and use what's within
Let the Spirit guide you coz
the Spirit is from Him
The Lord above knows what's in store for you
Keep the faith and it shall be revealed to you.
Love The Lord with all your heart, soul and mind
Open my eyes Lord, don't let me stay blind.
Let me always have an ear to hear

Keep me under your wing and
whom shall I fear?
Heal me of my infirmity and
let me turn from wrong
Let me practice patience and let me praise on.
I thank you Father for you are One
You are complete, and there
is nothing left undone.
Increase my faith and keep me steadfast
Wavering in my mind can never last
Give me a man who will take the lead
Your Oneness is an example of how to succeed.
Let our uniqueness be
complementary to one another
May I be an excellent wife and mother
May we both be the ultimate lovers
Love so strong there will be no other.

L.O.V.E

I know you love me
I can tell by the way you look at me.
Uncomfortable when around me
My aura astounds thee.
You make me feel good, compliment me all the
time
I'm your girl, I'm your woman,
mature like fine wine.
Your love is amazing
Protective like a glove, gentle as a dove.
I can't get enough
I feel so blessed to have you
I know that God loves me because you are a gift
To me from above,
L.O.V.E

Love.

My Prayer To Overcome

Lord show me the way and direct my paths.
Give me a clear vision, that I
may run with it but see
where I'm heading. Turn my ashes into beauty.
I have made a mess of things but I know that
you work all things together for my good. I
thank you for the privilege to come to you as
a daughter and that you will deal with me in
that way, because you chasten those whom
you love. Give me a fresh outpouring of your
Spirit and may our bond become stronger
day by day. Teach me how to love you. I
am saved by grace and not anything I have
done. Thank you Jesus that no matter what
I have done, you still love me, you died for
me love doesn't get any purer than that.
May I have victory over temptation
and overcome evil. I
don't know the plans you have
for my life but I thank you

that your ways are higher than
mine and they are always
the best. Help me not to be
influenced, but to be an
influence to others and a light to the world. I
know this prayer is not in vain and that
He hears me. I will trust in you yet.

Nobody's Perfect

It's like climbing up a hill of oil
No matter how much I climb I still fall.
I toil and toil and see no gain
If my plans fail I feel the pain.
Spiritually and physically I pray
it is well with my soul
To learn from life lessons is the ultimate goal
Don't wanna see the hole and still fall in
I need to go around this pit full of sin.
Set me free Father so I can win, I believe
I'm a winner and without you I am nothing.
May your spirit guide me forever and ever.
I choose to rise above
Not with hate, but with love.
Forget fears and wipe tears, move on
The Lord shall complete the work he has begun.
I will run the race and not refuse
To fight the battle I cannot lose.

Battlefield Of The Mind

It is important to make decisions and stick to them. The mind is a powerful tool and a battlefield. Each and everyday is a battle, we are living in a time of new age. Where everyone is reading self help books and following the law of attraction. Don't get me wrong the word of The Lord states 'For as he thinks about the cost, so is he' - Proverbs 23:7. So I am all for thinking positive thoughts, as we do tend to go where our mind goes. I just want to be lead also by the Spirit of God. To enjoy the fruit of your labor is the gift of God. We can accumulate as much as possible and still not be happy, but if we find fulfillment in what we do for a living and have a good work/life balance I think we are the most blessed of all. We need to maximize each moment and move on from past mistakes. Make a firm decision to make the right choices. Know that you were suppose to go through what you went through, to help you grow. God prunes you so that your fruit will remain. You will be a well-rounded person of character that has a depth of treasure to impart to the next generation.

You're (Black) History!

You say you're on my side
Say your down for me
Tell me what I like and promise me what I need.
You maybe should have tried this a year ago,
Coz I sure ain't blind to your lies no more.
You tried to have a hold on me, mash up my life
Used all the trigger words like 'baby' and 'wife'.
Tried to lock me down knowing all the while,
you were never serious, just playing around.
Sick and tired of the games you play
I've changed my mind starting from today.
I've seen your type before too many
times and I've been burnt
But this time I believe I've learnt.
To walk away because I deserve better
And better is out there I believe so I receive.
So I thank you for the hurt coz
one day you will miss me
And when you come back to me,
you'll just be black history!

Role Model?

Living from day to day
I wake up and feel the sunrays.
It's a gift that I've lived to see another day
We take for granted the guarantee of tomorrow
Take the right step and others will follow.
The pressure you feel when the spotlight is on
you
Little girls be watching everything you do.
Wanna dress like you
Wear their hair like you
And when they go off the rails their
parents wanna blame who?
...Me?
I can't help who I be
Started this journey in nineteen eighty three.
My message is we all have a purpose
Let's dig deeper, beneath the surface.
Let us not live our lives in haste

You could make it to the top but it could all be a waste.
Maximize the moments whatever will be will be
It's not about the destination
but about the journey.

Teach Others What We Have Survived

If not now...when?
Is the question always on my mind. I'm always
striving for the next goal to better myself. It's
like being part of a baseball team, gotta run to
the next base. I enjoy seeing what each day
unfolds for me. It's a beautiful feeling knowing
that I have the chance to make an impact on the
world. My ministry is teaching and I feel fulfilled
doing it. I'm glad that I have the opportunity to
meet many people and gain nuggets of wisdom
from the old, and life lessons from the young.
Yes from the young because they have things
to teach us also "Out of the mouth of babes".
We never stop learning. Our experiences are
there to shape and mold us but also to teach
others that we survived what they are going
through now, and that you can make it.

A Limited Edition

I am a limited edition.
Who else is like me? I have a mind of my
own and no one knows my thoughts.
Unless I choose to reveal them to you. I am
unique but simple an oxymoron at best.
I am an individual but yet I want to find someone
just like me. Really? Do I want someone as
complex or a polar opposite? I better make
up my mind quick. I ask many questions,
the majority is for a problem but what is the
solution? I need a solution ASAP. I am a star
my light cannot be imitated or duplicated. I am
amongst many other stars yes, but all shine a
different light. I am a young female and there's
a big world out there, waiting to be explored.
I am an eternal optimist, things can only get
better from my perspective. I am a pioneer I
take the lead and prepare the way for others. I
am a giver, I give of my heart and time because
time is precious. I am a mover, I refuse to be
stuck anywhere particularly in the past, keep
it moving regardless of what transpires.

Wisdom

Everyone needs a spiritual lift
The race is not for the swift.
The enemy is looking to sift,
whom he can as wheat,
But I stay bowed at the Most high's feet,
and with him I can see no defeat.
In his love there will be no separation,
much deeper than any penetration
I can get from a man.
A lot deeper than the mind can
understand Tighter than the Taliban,
and more loyal than a No. 1 fan.
You may go through pain, but to live is for Christ
And to die is gain.
You can't lose you can only win, When
you feel like the airs getting thin
Know that wisdom is the principle thing.

Looking For Love In All The Wrong Places

I've been looking for love in the
wrong place on earth
It's taken me a while to understand my worth.
Now I will seek your face and be fully immersed
In your love, I will seek your face first.
No longer will man try to value me
It can't compare to what the Father sees in me.
It will take a special man to fulfill my needs
To love me from my head to my feet.
Now I can be totally sure
Your spirit will lead to what I'm looking for.
A marriage bond so sacred and pure, but
only you can take me to that door.
I will wait and be happy with delay
"Delay is not denial 'you say.
Enjoy each moment of everyday,
"Wait"..He says "Just wait" He says.

Praise Him

Don't know where I'll be in 5 years or more
But what I do know is that I'll
be serving The Lord.
Whether I'm here or I'm on tour,
I know I'll give hardcore
Praise to the one who prolongs
my days, upon the land.
I lift my head, I lift my hands, I lift my voice
I lift the name of the one that's given me choice.
Of everlasting life and safety from the grave
Thank you Lord for coming to pave the way
Living in a world full of sin
You showed me that even though life's tempting
I can still have the victory.
Resist the Devil and what he
would suggest to me
Resist the Devil and the devil will flee.
The Almighty has got my back, Ever
need to know where your at.

Search the Word, better yet search your heart
From the start
He lived deep within.
Knowing you and knowing everything.

Questions

Life is getting better now I got my head
screwed on. It's so important to be
able to move on from bad situations,
but be grateful for the experience.
"We know that all things work together for good
for those who love God, to those who are called
according to his purpose" - Romans 8:28.
Thank God for every situation because there is
a divine plan. Along the way you are developing
character, resilience and tenacity. Being able
to stand through trials is fighting the good
fight of faith. It is extremely hard, and I have
had many of down days where I questioned
my faith and will definitely have more to
come. The comfort I have is knowing that
God will provide a way of escape from every
temptation and that Jesus paved the way by
overcoming the world. Our job is to continue

shining our light in the world so that God can be glorified, so if you are thinking, why am I in this situation? Why don't God just take us away from all of this? Just know that through every good act you display to others, they have experienced the Spirit of God that lives in you.

Balance

A gentle summer breeze is a
whisper through the trees
yet has the power to force nature out
of it's resting place. Invisible to the eye
unless you are in motion, a very humble
position is the wind the force of nature.
How lonely it must be to be fire. The sun
gives tremendous light but it stands alone,
a ball of energy that enriches the earth
but an inch closer it will scorch it.
How gentle fresh water can be, so nourishing to
the thirsty soul, was probably the first element
to exist and is so vast. You can break solid
iron, put out fire and may have swallowed up
many in your ocean, yet you are vital for life.
The earth you are constantly walked upon
and receive the dead, yet you yielded the first
man and continue to encase seed which bear
many a fruit. Guess my point is even with

the powerful elements there is a balance of good and bad. Don't think of yourself more highly than you ought to think but think of yourself with sober judgment. Balance is a fundamental principle of life. Whatever you give you must take, whatever you sow, you must reap, and everything in moderation Two ends of the spectrum - meet me in the middle.

A Learning Curve

I hope she's worth the pain
Cos once I'm over you I'll never cry again.
I'm not bitter I'm just saying
I hope you're prepared for what
is around the corner.
It was a gamble to love you and I took that risk
In the hope you'd surprise me
and be better than this.
I take away the positive, which is that
I'll surely learn, when you pour out your
love you're bound to be burned.
So I pick up the pieces of my
broken heart and offer
To my God who is my legitimate lover.
Who is able to mend and bring me back to life
And assure me of the promise that I'll be a wife.
To someone who can love me
and value my worth.
To see me through the eyes of The Lord.
To cherish and protect me like my God.
I know that The Lord has a perfect plan for
me and I will hold onto His promises.

His promises renew my life. It picks me up
from the dirt. He delivers me from wicked.
Evil men who are liars and smooth talkers.
I will rise again from the ashes, and trust
and believe that my Father is good at all
times. You are able to do exceedingly,
abundantly and above all I can ask or think.

Same Person, Different Face

Father, allow me stay focused on my goals. It is through affliction that I really learn that you are always with me, even though you're silent. I have learnt in this world suffering can be a blessing, because in these times you are truly near to those who are broken hearted. Allow me to learn from my mistakes, you know the ones I ALWAYS repeat. Deliver me from evil in whatever shape or form. People will probably wonder why every other page is about God or a man...well first of all *out of the abundance of the heart the mouth speaks*, and second my secret is out. It's always some guy (or waste man) that tries to distract me from the goals I have set for myself in life. I need to just focus on my God and the plan he has for my life. Tired of seeing

the ditch and still falling into it. I need to do something different and flee unrighteousness. Allow me to discern unrighteousness Father. Your Spirit is a light in my soul searching all the dark places in my life.

I'm Focused

Just when I got my mind right... that's
when you wanna come back
Forget that, you will never get that
Good loving, warm huggin',
good treatment again.
It's like you know when I forget about you
No longer looking out for your phone calls.
That's when you wanna pursue
me and drive by my house
I'm getting tired of this game of cat and mouse.
You made your choice from the beginning
and now you wanna change?
Telling me the things I wanted to
hear in our former days
Well my mind is in a happy place
When I was with you, you thought I
wasn't good enough to chase.
Guess you've had a lot of time to think
You've realized I'm a Queen and
the captain of the ship.
I must admit you nearly got me,
I nearly fell for your lies

Broke my heart into so many
pieces but still I will survive.
I'm just gonna do me, that may
come as a surprise
But I'm better off without you
so I can heal inside.

Baffled!

Why do you keep coming back? I really
don't know. Have you come to your
senses and realized you want more?
That there's nothing out there
of quality and substance
Finally realized you wanna be a husband?
It's funny how many beautiful
faces you cannot pass by
Rather juggle many women and
tell a whole pack of lies
It's not the face but the
character you remember.
That awesome experience
from winter to summer
That wholesome girl and all-round kinda lover.
Who gives you her all but
knows what she's worth
If she walks away it will be a
lonely place on earth.
She runs through your mind on a daily basis
In the middle of a desert she's your oasis.
The one who makes your life complete

Upon seeing her, your heart skips a beat.
When you're away you just wanna be near her
You wanna heal her when she's weak.
She's the one you have a deep
connection with The one that makes
you question is this what love is?

Is The World Becoming Colder?

Is it just me or is the world becoming cold?
Maybe I'm exaggerating, maybe I'm getting old.
Maybe I'm just different, or my horse is too high
But how can people walk past
you without saying Hi?
How can you offer a lift and charge for going
the same way? Why do you talk behind my
back but in my face have nothing to say? How
can you have neighbors but don't know their
name? How can you say you love me like family
yet don't treat me the same? If you don't like
me, tell me, there's no need to act, I prefer
you be upfront and just present the facts.
You see me coming behind you and you don't
hold open the door, Where's your sense of
morals don't anyone have manners anymore?
Why have women settled for a man who thinks
it's ok to cheat? Say you want a strong man but
put up with him who's weak. Have no patience
to wait for anyone so we go on trips alone.

A world of isolation, individualism has grown.
We are so consumed with self we can do it
all on our own. Then we moan when we are
single but look at the seeds we've sown.
Maybe we should cherish the moments,
the ones of give and take.
Is the world becoming colder?
No, I guess I'm just wide awake.

Happy

Happy is what I choose to be, if you
see me laughing that's just me.
I love to see beauty and things that look nice.
Gold, jewels, gems and ice.
Like to be in nice surroundings
cars and buildings too.
Like to enjoy the fruit of my labor
and experience them with you.
You are the one I wanna be with, the one
who makes me smile. When I think of all I've
been through, it was worth it all the while.
Love the experience of freedom I thank The
Lord above for giving me wisdom as wise
as a serpent but as harmless as a dove.
Hope my words are a blessing to all
who hear and read, may these words
empower all with the ability to succeed.

A Test of Love

I still choose to love you coz
there's hope in me yet
I can forgive what you've done
but I'll never forget.
To love you is something I cannot regret
It's better to have loved and lost
than to always reject.
My feelings towards you were ambivalent
A bit like the equivalent of the British
weather, but the more time we spend
together I see a deep love unfold.
A strong connection that will last till we're old
The test of our love is refined like gold
Like a bridge over troubled water
our story will be told.
Could it be it's happened to me?
I've found the one I love, was this meant to be?
An example of endurance and desire
to succeed. Have I finally found a
man who will take the lead?
What's different about me? I
believe in happy endings

Not the fairly tale type but the
story you keep defending.
Protect precious love because long
suffering is what it's made of.
Trouble produces a precious jewel
once everything is weighed up
The good treasure is in heaven that's where
everything is laid up
When I need guidance I make
sure that I stay prayed up.

So Grateful

I wake up each morning with a thankful heart
Think of fallen soldiers that had to depart.
Fresh air that I breathe I see
the birds in the trees
Give thanks to the Father for watching over me.
Eyes that see clearly, the use of my hands
Got strength in my bones in order to stand.
Don't have much jewelry, don't
have much money
I'm free in my mind and that's all that I need.
When I see the light see the light of
day, makes me wanna say...
"I'm so grateful to be alive"
When I see the light see the light of
day makes me wanna say...
"I'm so grateful to be alive".
In life we take small things for granted
But a tree was once a seed that was planted.
Grows so tall but was buried in darkness
Made it through the struggle,
experience contrasted.
It's in these things that we learn life's lessons

That, in everything we can receive a blessing.
Appreciate life each moment each second,
That is true happiness don't you reckon?

The Storm

Out of pain come peace, passion and pleasure
In times of darkness is where
you find your treasure
A real diamond has to go through pressure
If I'm going through a storm
does it mean I'm lesser?
God is with me through it all
He may be silent but he hears your call.
Make your request known no matter how small
He'll pick you up the second time you fall
The third, fourth, fifth and sixth time too
He's not just staring from a birds eye view.
Like a game of chess wondering
which piece to move next
No, as promised he keeps guiding each step.
He is by your side he is omnipresent
He will look after you, if he takes
care of the pheasant

And how much more are you than they?
He watches every waking day
So give thanks and praise to the Almighty, yes!
And each and every day just
know that you are blessed.

It's Complicated!

"I just want to be happy with
you", that's what you said
But your actions are contrary
or non existent instead.
I wanna believe you coz I want us to be happy
too, Is it so hard to change the things you do?
Wanting different results but doing
the same thing is insanity
Looking out for yourself and
admiring you is vanity.
If we don't work this out I can feel a calamity
Are you the be all and end all not indefinitely.
My friends keep telling me to leave
But being with you makes me
happy if you can believe.
When we are together all we do is fight
I'm like a moth to a flame blinded by the light.
Can't things just run smooth without the drama?
And why you gotta be someone's
else baby father?
It's messed up that I still want you all the same
I'm being honest but I think your playing games.

If I'm such a prize to be won then
why can't I find the one?
Just leading a simple, happy life under the sun
Why is all so complicated?
And I know it's not just me
It's happened since the beginning
look at Adam and
Eve.
I'm willing to be happy in everything I do
But just once can't it be too good
and actually be true?

I See You In My Dreams...

I see you in my dreams, if only they were reality. We're really enjoying life and each other. We know how to get along and handle day to day affairs together. The household runs smooth because we are a team. Working together to achieve our goals, raising a family, our first child of many is born. She has your eyes and my smile a perfect mix. He has your temperament and my complexion.
Our children are a mirror of us,
a walking reflection.

The Cure And The Cause

The cure and the cause, you're
my forbidden desire
I could choose to walk away
or dance with the fire.
When will I ever learn, that to play
with fire you'll always get burned.
Don't ignore the facts but have
the power to discern
That people can take advantage
of your kindness.
Living in a world of wickedness and self gain
To live in love is definitely a long suffering game.
But to love is what I must do all the same,
It's not just my nature but the
meaning of my name.
If we don't show love then who will be the light?
If we don't show love how do we
judge wrong from right?
We walk in darkness but
righteousness is in clear sight

The choice to do good or bad is a daily fight.
Keep my foot from all unrighteousness
Lord. Let me use my words as a sword.
To fight and withstand the evil day
Thank you for guiding and showing me the way.

Super Woman

I'm an excellent wife, and a great mother.
A fantastic cook and a great lover.
I work hard and my house is clean
I could be Superwoman so it seems.
I stay strong even when I'm weak, I stand
up for what's right to keep the peace.
A calm exterior but my mind runs deep
I like to lead but to God I'm a sheep.
My cup overflows, my well is not dry
My hope of your promises goes beyond the sky.
My heart of flesh is encased in steel, I'm
open and honest, love keeping it real.
There is more to me than what meets the eye
Will you dare to love me as much as I?

I Hear Your Voice

The sound of your voice is whisper.
When it comes to the future you give a picture.
A vision of hope that defies circumstance
Makes you wanna laugh, cry, sing and dance.
It's so far from what you've imagined
and yet straight away it's like the
opposite has happened.
Then I start to disbelieve what you have said
And begin to think that maybe
it was all in my head.
Maybe it was just my voice or
the voice of the Devil,
He shows up every time we enter a new level
But when I start to doubt, I lay it down
I speak to myself and say "His love abounds."
I wrestle with these thoughts everyday
Show me how to love the right way.
Then the test comes and then I fail
But evil will certainly not prevail.

The Fight of Faith

I feel in my head there's an intrusion
Why am I in a state of confusion?
Is what I'm seeing an illusion?
I need a spiritual infusion.
Lord help me on this roller coaster
My emotions are topsy turvy.
When I feel like this I question are you there?
Am I on the right path or have you deserted me?
I hope not because I need you more than ever.
Faith comes by hearing and I hear your voice
I know you are near.
I feel your presence, you are so real,
Realer than my reality
Holding my hand and walking
me through the darkness.
Thank you for your assurance Father,
in every waking day I will serve you
I will give you all the praise
because you alone are good.
If only I could be a fraction of what you
are Lord Nevertheless I will rejoice in my
broken spirit just because you are God.

You Have To Go Through

You have to go through the fire
to be refined as pure gold.
You have to walk through the
darkness to get to the light.
You have to fly through the clouds
to get to clear sky's.
The shepherd David walked
through the valley of
the shadow of death.
Jonah went through the whale.
Jesus went through the pit of hell.
Moses went through the wilderness.
They all came out the other side
victorious! I shall be victorious,
because I walk through with God.
I let go of all my sorrows and my
burdens and release them to you.
It's a fact that God's grace and mercy
shall follow me wherever I go.

Go through, walk through and don't stop till you reach the other side.

The Journey

I'm waiting at the bus stop I'm hasty to know
The destination I'm heading
for, where should I go?
You order my steps and you
make my path straight
But why do I always find it so hard to wait?
Always on the move and want
to rush to the next spot
I'm in the race of life excited
for the next stop, but it's
not the destination or the end that's the goal.
It's the journey along the way
because it's you I get to know.
Ever been somewhere far, so
long you wanna sleep?
Alone it can be boring but it's
the company you keep.
Along the way there's so much more to be learnt
You give nuggets of wisdom and
knowledge, that can't be burnt,
You say I'm with you always,
even till the end of time

It's not in my greatest moments but in
the darkness where you shine.
So even though you're waiting,
or surrounded by darkness
He may be silent but he keeps
his promises regardless.

The Mystery of Relationships

The enemy's biggest operation is division.
So many relationships are broken
because they can't envision
Walking together and agreeing
to full participation
We want everything quick, the
microwave generation.
We have so many independent
women, I think we've gone wrong
Although I know we enjoyed
singing that Beyoncé song.
But now it's made a hole in
societies moral fabric
Men cheat out in the open and
their lies are so elaborate.
You know that we are coming to the
final hour, because relationships no
longer have any staying power.
I guess this is what it means to
be the salt of the earth,

The road to destruction is wide, but
do you know what your worth?
You are the light of the world
so withstand the evil day
Things will be hard but keep loving
anyway. If people don't remember
the things that they should
When they think of you they
should remember the good.

Visions

I believe that what your word says is true. Right
now it's the opposite but I need to go through.
At the end of the tunnel there's
a light that leads to,
The happiest moments that happen
once in a blue moon.
The spirit inside me is excited in advance,
And spontaneously makes me
want to sing and dance,
Because the spirit knows what
the flesh can't see
I see glimpses at times in visions and dreams
But sometimes I don't always
know what they mean.
So I've decided to let go and
leave it all in your hands
Take each day as it comes and
hope to understand.
Each step that you reveal to me is a blessing
If I practice this daily it will keep
me from second-guessing.
Because life is a journey full of great lessons.

So I keep walking with you in
prayer and thanksgiving.
I will praise your name still in
the land of the living
Each sunrise I see is a miracle you're bringing.

Frustrated Feelings

Spend my days just thinking about you
Wondering if you're thinking of me too.
Imagining if we did make our first child
I picture you getting gassed with a big smile.
First impression, felt I already knew you
And every time we met was always a new you,
And even though I think you
know that it's meant to be
You'd rather be miles apart, far away from me.
If I'm the one then why does
it make you scared?
It doesn't matter if it's my feelings
that you wanna spare
My emotions will still be intact,
But don't lie and tell me that
I've made no impact.
On your life, on your thoughts, on
your time, on your mind.
Hoping at some point we could press rewind
Every tune, perfume, and emotionally
Somehow or some way will remind you of me.

I'm Different

Yes I'm different.
My skin is dark.
The colour is a rich deep
brown tone like the soil.
Hair tightly curled like the number nine.
Which I'm sure is divine.
A member of the only people in the
world with the hair they call fro.
No need to be different just look at me though.
I'm brown like a crayon fresh from Crayola.
Natural brown from the earth no artificial mix
Just a pure natural tone from the earth's core.

Encourage Yourself

Learn to encourage yourself. Through all the hurts, anguish and pain, pack it into a little bag and move on. Leaving the bag behind. I say a little bag because God said they are "light afflictions". The beauty of walking with God is that he is faithful on a daily basis. His love is what renews my spirit and when I run out of words to say his spirit speaks through me. I thank you Father that this is the time in which you are the nearest to me. It's in the dark places where I discover you. When the children of Israel were receiving the Ten Commandments they didn't want to hear your voice because they were terrified. But Moses spoke to them and then returned to the dark cloud where you were. Suddenly I'm not afraid because you are the light but you are with us in dark places. You are the great and terrible God and there is none like you. You are mighty and you give gifts to those who ask, yes you give freely. Your word is powerful

and unbreakable, never returning to you void
but setting out from eternity to accomplish
what you have decreed. Thanks for helping
me to change by the renewing of my mind.

Just To Say…
Thank You

This is just to say thank you for your marvelous works. Each and everyday I get a little closer to knowing you. I can never know you fully but it's amazing that you even want to know me, and fellowship with me. The lowly, a mere mortal, but like new parents you enjoy your own creation. I pray that you will give us a creative spirit. We should strive to be creative and innovative. Let us realize the power of our words and speak things into existence. These words that we speak are spirit and they are life, so let us speak and meditate on good things. Immerse us in your love and guidance. Use us as vessels to speak through. Allow us to speak words that inject hope and encouragement. Words are so important use them wisely or let them be few.

Who Is Like You?

Your thoughts towards me are good all the time
Your majesty you are so divine.
Who is like you? Who is good? No one, But
yet you watch over everything under the sun.
You keep me from evil, my personal protection
My heart you test, my spirit's inspection.
You enable me to become a reflection, of
you to become your treasured collection.
The way you love me is beyond comprehension
When I'm far from you I can feel the tension
The pull is like elastic I spring right back
When I realize I have nothing
and evidently in lack.
In your presence is fullness of joy
Enough to thwart the enemy's ploy.
Everyday my mind is a battlefield, but you
are my fortress, you are my shield.

I'm Here To Inspire

My tongue is sharp like a razor
If you don't know me my names Miss
Frazer.
If you're not here to learn see you later.
How long will it take ya?
Make ya, or break ya
You are the creator.
I'm here to inspire
Kindle a flame to ignite a great fire
Until I retire.
Stop music? Never.
I hope that together we'll always
endeavor,
To have self discipline
In the world that we living in.
That's hard when you wanna do
your own thing. It's only common sense
and this is no pretense,
To be the best, you have to practice excellence.

The Spirit Moves

Thank you father, everlasting Savior
Thank you for challenging and
correcting my behavior.
I'm glad that in your sight I have found favor
Thank you for giving rest from my heavy labor.
In your love there will never be
condemnation for a daughter like me.
When my sorrow floods like
the waves of the sea
You say I'll bear fruit like the leaves of a tree.
Before my mothers womb you
knew me from the start
Like a surgeon you carefully
mend my broken heart.
Like the Potters clay I'm a work of art
May you abide in me and never depart.
In times of sadness I will rejoice, because
it's in these times that I hear your voice
You order my steps but give me choice

When I fall in the pit my spirit you hoist.
From me you will withhold no good thing
You watch me grow like a flower in spring
Your goodness I will share and sing
My Lord of lords and King of kings.

Who Is The Greatest?

Give me wisdom in order to teach
My ear I incline, I will lay at your feet.
To listen to your every Word
My purpose will always be to serve.
Yes haven't you heard the latest? That to
serve on earth you will be the greatest.
The greatest In heaven, like
Jesus he led by example
Exalted in heaven his treasures are ample.
To love is to serve and that is the key
To put an end to war and to poverty.
I delight in your way for I know you are right
In a world full of darkness we are the light.
Eternal optimist I will hope in you yet
I refuse to be sad and refuse to regret.
Your love for me cannot be measured by length
I will wait upon you because
you are my strength.

Write The Vision

Write your vision and make it plain.
Once you have be patient and wait.
For it will surely come and won't delay
I'm a witness that he works in
mysterious ways.
From the stores of my spirit your words overflow
Inscribed upon my heart is
your word that I know.
The eyes and ears are a gate.
What flows out of you? Is it love or hate?
Guaranteed that's what you've been feeding off,
And eventually it escapes the body like a cough,
My broken spirit you cherish
You chasten me so that I won't perish.
You give me new hopes and dreams
Let my doubts evaporate like steam.

Facades

We walk around with a smile, trying to mask
All the problems we face more
numerous than the stars
Underneath this earth suit is a heart full of scars
A hidden anger more fiery than mars.
But when it comes to hope I'm
a prisoner behind bars
Because I know that not all seasons will last.
I know the plans you have for me are so vast
To give a future more greater than the past
I trust in your ways and on you I will cast
My burdens, you will take as long as I ask
You will rescue me and answer me fast
To walk with you is not a burdensome task
If I don't have love, my prayer sounds like brass
Here for a moment then wither like grass
Wickedness is prevalent but
your love will surpass
The evil day your word will outlast
You see everything, to you I'm a glass
Life is a teacher and I'm a student in your class.

Love and Pain
Is Gain

What is love?
I'm learning everyday, so far I've been in pain.
Pain and fear of leaving myself wide open for
someone who doesn't deserve it.
Love is power and strength and God is love.
It takes power and strength to love someone
beyond what they deserve and it's this love
that causes me to want to do good. When
I think about the goodness of The Lord it
makes me cry and makes me happy. If God
loved me the way I loved people I would be
doomed. I ask you Father that you show me
how to love. I know the situation I'm in is a test
of my strength and power of love. Guide me
through this Father, I need you more than ever.
Love is a sacrifice. To die to self is gain. I
lay my thoughts before you Lord and I ask
that you influence me to do the right thing.

Connections

Reflection.
As I'm looking for direction
I realize life is about making deep connections.
Eye contact an indicator of inspection
I can sense the truth no need for any questions.
When you pour out your heart and I
see vulnerability Enables me to do the
same, it creates sensitivity Conversation
makes me aware of my abilities
Explore my mind and take note of its agility.
I'd rather see you in person
just so I can be near ya,
Even that's getting harder with
the rise of social media
Instead of calling we text because it's easier
Need information? We just go on Wikipedia.
Be aware of the relationships your severing
The bible says don't forsake
fellowship my brethren.
But it's not good that man should be alone
And yet so many single people
be living on their own.

Cherish connections, you don't
have to let everyone in
But recognize your confidants and the positive
they bring. They are the ones that build you
up and support you when you're down.
The ones that make you feel so much
happier when they're around
The ones that help to keep you
fighting through another day
Who help to change your perspective
and see things another way.
Cherish deep connections, raise
your glass make a toast
More than anything connection
is what we need most.

FBK

I'm starting to feel that Facebook
should be renamed 'Go
Compare'
All it does is create the illusion life isn't fair.
You're blessed but it makes you
notice things you haven't got
But if you truly counted your blessings
you'd see you have a lot.
I think that watching people's lives
is something we need to quit
Because all we do is make social
comparisons and end up feeling sick.
Be honest with yourself are
reality shows really reality?
So don't you think all these
filtered pictures are vanity?
Don't get me wrong I'm on the bandwagon too
But viewing a slide show doesn't
mean I know you.
In fact I feel the opposite, it's
a way for us to hide

How many people put a post of
what they really feel inside?
My husbands having an affair, my
sister changed her name to Mike
I've put so much weight, would that get a like?
I'm not saying the whole world needs to know
your business, I'm just asking questions, coz I
really need to quiz this, It's worrying that you
have to write a post of how happy you is
Because if you really were, would
you even have time for this?
Yes photos can capture the time we live in
But experience the moment, by
cherishing truly living.

My Man

You're a mature man
Not an insecure man
The type to clean floors and open doors
type man.
A strongman
Good taste in song man
The kinda type to admit he's wrong man.
A healing man
Paint the ceilings man
The type to share your feelings man.
Eyes glistening man
An envisioning man
At the end of the day he's a listening man.
A courting man
Hold the fort type man
When I'm down you're a supporting man.
He can govern man
Use the oven man
Not afraid to show he's a loving man.

No More Excuses

So many beautiful women are
waiting for that man
We bend over backwards trying to understand,
Him and his flaws,
The cause of his demise.
He's the way he is cause mum
left when he was five
Or he grew up in poverty
His dad left when he was ten.
But we've all had a ruff start my friend
Yes we all have and if you didn't you will
Growing through trials is a God given skill.
So if women can be strong then why can't he?
We can deal with our issues
by becoming a team.
Not making excuses for a messed up beginning
To establish roots you must keep on digging
And digging until with love you overcome
But at the first sign of trouble
we seem to want to run.
I can see how a reflection of goodness
would make you want to flee

But don't be intimidated walk and agree.
Want to be better for yourself in essence?
Those you look up to be in their presence
Birds of a feather flock together
Relationships help to unlock your treasure.
Yes we are here to help each other grow
But if you walk away now, will you ever know?

Relationship Myths

The perfect man is a myth.
Your first encounter wasn't epic
The old trick of divide and conquer
has become an epidemic.
Burned, battered and bruised are
the war scars we choose
Because we always stay with someone
that we're afraid to lose.
And evidently we start the
game of self sabotage
Like a montage, we collect
memories of lovers past
And compare a current love
even when they don't ask
And jump right into another
relationship when it don't last
Coz were afraid of being alone in case we
start to analyze ourselves and really start
to ponder, is it me? Do I need help?
Am I too picky? Nah it's not me it's
him and it's not him it's her
What did I ever see in you in
the first place? Ergh!!,

But for the moment you were
perfect never realizing as such
That to sustain a relationship goes
beyond looks and touch
Because if that's the only reason
your bond to feel disdain
After a while you'll realize that
the key word is sustain
Can you endure when the road gets tough?
I'm not just talking lip service or calling my bluff
Selling dreams or painting a picture for right now
I'm saying will you still love me long after the
wow, factor has left and the magic ain't there?
The kids have left the house, and
we're in a rocking chair
You don't stay because you have
to but coz you really care
You're firm in your decision and
neither here or there
Double minded and blinded to what
other people think No let's stay together
coz our hearts are in sync.

Trust, Believe And Be Still

Love is as strong as death.
When you're gone it feels like I have nothing left.
Much more than hugging and kissing
A break up feels like something is missing.
A part of you is gone and as hard
as you try to move on,
The healing process is long.
The heartache is major.
Even for my worst enemy I
wouldn't wish to trade ya.
Go through this again, nah, I
think I'd rather be in labor
The pain cuts so deep, further than the
white meat enough tears to soak the
pillow, mattress and white sheets.
And no one is exempt coz pain knows no name
And if I was negative I'd say
love is a losing game
All the same despite what I said
above I'd do it all again

Coz I know true love is out
there, it's not if, it's when.
And yes give yourself time to mend
Don't just blend into another relationship
tryin to pretend that your happy
Coz the same thing will happen again
and you'll end up feeling crappy.
Wait upon The Lord, you'll get to see his will
Wait upon The Lord, trust believe and be still.

Looking Forward

Things are looking up and I'm
excited about what's to come
It's summer outside but the
winter has been long.
I'm talking about the seasons of life
It happens in every area, I
sense the brink of spring
A new beginning makes me merrier.
My spirit overflows with the joy I'm about to see
Because the Spirit knows and
goes ahead of me.
Gently guiding me through the
coldest winter ever,
Will you leave me or forsake me
your Word says never!
I treasure the hope of something new
Novelty, innovation, brings inspiration
In your presence is a new sensation
Took the road less traveled I
found I've discovered
The secrets to life you've
revealed and uncovered.

Like a mother you withhold no
good thing from your child
My heart is glad and when I think of you I smile
Knowing you were with me all the while
When I was weary you carried me another mile.
Your promises enlighten
My spirit brightens
Just when I think hope is lost I see the horizon.

Teacher

I am a teacher, a public speaker
I am here to teach and guide
To nourish the hungry mind
Through music you can unwind.
I'm here to draw out your potential
The possibility of seeing things another way
Unlocking talents and putting them on display
Establishing relationships and building trust,
In the world of education knowledge is a must
To discuss world issues and
music that is ageless,
My passion is evident, overflows it's contagious,
It's more than being recognized or being famous
It's a love of transference a
quality that's gracious.
It's more than just a service or
helping those who yearn
The best teachers don't know everything
but are still willing to learn.

Opposition

Fight the good fight of faith
Believe what you can't see and wait.
Doubt steps in with a question, a suggestion,
That perhaps you didn't receive that word mate.
The enemy comes to kill, steal, and destroy
His ploy is to steal your promise.
But pay homage to the one
that is greater than he
Who whispered doubt in the garden to Eve.
Take your shield of faith, give thanks and pray
Not just for the moment but do this everyday.
Every minute and every chance that you get
It's closer than you think even
though you can't see it yet
It's a fight it's a struggle and a battle of the mind,
Be rooted and grounded and
eventually you'll find
That your faith is growing it's being exercised.
Opposition is a blessing, it's a test for the wise.
It should come as no surprise,
when it comes don't ask how
As soon as you receive a promise
believe and receive now.

Most Faithful

Great are your ways and your
works are marvelous
I will give praise till the end of my days
You give me strength and allow me to be
victorious
You give me length of days so glorious.
You speak to my spirit daily
Never leave me nor forsake me.
Empower me with the tools to withstand evil
Enlighten me in the school of life
You give me nuggets of knowledge
and wisdom is like gold
Allow me to cherish these treasures till I am old.
And gray hairs grace the whole of my head
I've never seen your chosen
ones begging for bread
You have been faithful even when I have not
You are the CEO you're always on top,
Ahead of the game, for-seer of the future
Make me laugh you have a real sense of humor

Friends

Whoever is friendly to others has many friends
It's an investment of give and
take call it dividends.
We Like each other beyond style and trends
Although that could be part of it
I like the things you have but I don't desire it.
In fact I love the fact that we like the same things
Our common interests is what brings us
together, do you make me feel insecure? Never!
Coz a true friend will always have
your best interests at heart
They tell you the truth even if it does leave scars
Any disagreements you should
be able to get past
Our friendship stays the same no
matter when I saw you last
They inspire you to be the best you, you can be
They give as much as they
take, balance...you see
Keeps me on my toes and doesn't
make me feel nervous

But someone who can explore
what's beneath the surface
It hurts when you share your
deepest secrets just to find
They were never really with you in
fact they were behind your back,
or crawling through the grass
seeking your demise
They can laugh in your face
and smile with their eyes
But thank God for discernment, the
gift to see beyond the veil
I need discernment like the blind need Braille
Allow me to leave behind
friendships that are stale
Recognize your confidants
cause they will never fail.

Let It Go

My head is barely above water
I feel like to sink and go under
To let go and be released from
all the pressures of life
Let God take the steering wheel
Since I have no idea where I'm going
I pray my faith will not fail but that
you will strengthen my mind.
That I will not walk by what I can
see but what I believe
You can exceed my thoughts of
happiness and expectation
So I lay it all down before you Father,
This load is far too heavy to carry.
Thank you for every blessing you
have given me under the sun,
Strengthen me and allow me to press on,
To follow where you lead and to
be sensitive to your voice
And help me to know that every
experience is ordained by you.

Zodiac

As fast as the wind rushing through the trees
Leaders of the zodiac meet Aries.
Head strong like an ox, materials things are us
Bull in a China shop meet Taurus.
Communication is everything,
many friends have I
Can sometimes be fickle meet Gemini.
As deep as the ocean, intuition is the answer,
Switch moods like the weather meet Cancer.
Need to be noticed, heads turn as I go
Hate being ignored, meet Leo.
Life's full of drama, life's full of woe
But love to fix the problem, meet Virgo.
Can't make up my mind, I switch like a lever
Love to get dolled up introducing Libra.
My mind runs deep, if your
shallow youv'e gots to go
My stare is really piercing call me Scorpio.
Travel the world in a flash, lots
of issues to discuss
Need to work on that tact, I'm Sagittarius.

Lover of money, work from dusk till dawn,
Need stability, call me Capricorn.
Very cerebral, in fact quite hilarious
Love doing it my way only, I'm Aquarius.
Cry me a river, cry me a sea,
I'm original, meet Pisces.

On The Right Track

Ever feel like in life this is what
you was meant to do?
I feel like I'm on the right track, it's déjà vu.
My mind and spirit has been here before
It's amazing the premonitions that we
have. Knowing what is ahead is a skill
something that only God can reveal.
Your ways and works are marvelous because
I am in your hands every step of the way.
I will give thanks and praise, my daily
sacrifice as this is my lot in life.
To whom much is given much is required
I thank you for this stage of my life in which
there is much to learn and there is much to gain.
I thank you that I have the pitcher and that I am
a lender not a borrower. You have blessed me
tremendously and I just want to take this time
to acknowledge you Father, the Most High,
without you I can do nothing. I really mean
nothing. Thanks for loving me all the same. For
leading and directing my paths. Keep me on
the right track Lord so I can serve you forever

Music Is My Life

Music.
Music is my life.
Releases stress and gets rid of strife.
Changes my mood it is food for the soul
Keeps me young and fresh I can never get old
With music my life it's a sound track
Them 90s tunes take me right back
Listening to Lil Kim, Biggie and Tupac
Lyrics stick in my head like blue tac.

Marriage Vows

Just an average 30 year old female from
London.
Searching for the solution to that
number one problem.
Commitment, exclusivity that ends in
marriage and a few baby carriages
For better or for worse, we always want
the better, but seem to get the latter
We always wanna quit before we
get to the heart of the matter.
But the reason why I chose you
and perhaps you chose me
Is because we have the endurance and tenacity
We refuse to quit and give up on each other
Want no other because your my kind of lover
Not perfect but we walk to see
things through till the end
A constant friend, our relationship
you protect and defend.

So Young, So Free

When I wake I feel energy inside me
Through the day I know your
Spirit always guides me
Knowing love and good will is what inspires me
It's who I am.
I just wanna give joy to all my people
Keep my head up and don't focus on the evil
Negativity around you can be lethal
So leave it behind.

Coz I'm so young and I'm so free
When I'm down ain't nobody gonna stop me
Gonna reach the top I'll never give up
Always striving for the best in me

It's so easy to not wanna do the right thing
But I seem to dodge all the
hurdles that life brings
When life is hard and things get
rough that's when my soul sings
I take the rough with the smooth.

Always give thanks never
despise small beginnings
And in my head I know these
words are always ringing
When you're about to quit don't stop
that's when you're winning
It's just character building It's only for a season.

A Prayer of Thanksgiving

I thank you Father for life and breath and the
opportunity to see another day. I'm grateful
that throughout my life you have been with
me and I have been a witness to the fact that
you are good all the time and you withhold no
good thing from me. You don't just allow me
to see your goodness but experience it first
hand. You have truly sustained me and have
been faithful to me at all times even when I've
been fickle. It is truly a battle to renew my mind
but I pray that I will be transformed. I pray that
like the lotus flower that grows in mud, I will be
transformed into a being without blemish, in fact
I thank you that you see me that way already.

Alone or All One?

Tell me if you think that man
was made to be alone?
It was for that reason God formed
Eve from Adams bone.
Although they made a mess of things
and the seeds of sin were sown
At least they had each other, through
tribulations they've grown.
Ultimately I have to admit that
two is better than one
Even the moon stands alone but
it's opposite is the sun.
Even fire needs air or the flame can't
live on just like faith without works
is dead being alone is no fun.
My purpose is to bear fruit and
teach the next generation
Endure hardship till the end as
there will be many tribulations.
But nevertheless like waiting
for a train at the station
I anticipate, I wait, The Lord is my fixation.

He knows the way that I should
take like a game of chess
When the battle is raging you provide
me with rest. Whichever age or
stage I know I am blessed
But save me from the battle of singleness.

The Gift of Life

What a beautiful day to have a clean
slate and start all over again.
To share of myself with the world, and
give words of encouragement and
bless those who are less fortunate.
To give thanks to the Most high for
length of days and to be happy in
this present state of mind.
Thank you for peace that goes beyond my
understanding and the ability to enjoy the fruits
of my labor. To experience enjoyment on earth
is a gift from God and I just want to take this
time to give thanks and praise to you. Thank
you for your guiding Spirit who leads me in
the paths of righteousness. We each have
a choice each day to do the right thing even
when we don't want to. Lord give me strength.

The Opposites In Nature

It is important to have balance.
A balanced diet.
A balanced lifestyle. Opposites
in nature produce balance,
The moon and the sun
The sea and the sky
The birds and the fish
Fire and water
Male and female
Love and hate (or indifference).

The Essence of Me

The essence of me is essentially me,
It's not just this outta earth suit you see
My words will go on for generations,
And words are spirit they are also life.
May your essence always be
encouraging and positive.
So much so that you cannot be replaced.
Make your mark on the earth long after
people have forgotten your face.
A good name is worth more than gold
Strive to protect it.

Being In Love

I'm a sucker for love, I have so much to give
The world is full of colour and everything is
So beautiful when you're in love, makes you feel
All warm inside and you go to work with a smile.
When you think about your one and only
Knowing that this world is no longer lonely
But you have that special someone with
whom you can share, a world of happiness.
Having someone to care for is a real
blessing, It's in these moments that we
give of ourselves and learn to grow.
You are my partner, a mirror my reflection
My opposite but we fit and I don't know if it was
God's intention, But where I lack you
meet the need and I am made to help.
We succeed because we realize
it's not just about self
But about self sacrifice, not keeping
any record of wrongs
Let's fulfill the mystery of two becoming one.

Learning Curve
– Part Two

Ups and downs, twists and turns
The curves of life is why we learn
Could you experience height if you weren't
in a pit? Still I will survive, with tears in
my eyes from the ashes I will rise.
I put myself out there whole-heartedly
My intentions were always pure
Giving my all, to love, cherish and adore
Rejected of man but loved by God.
The foolish mistakes I've made enable
me to become more awake.
Works like a torch in a dark pit of snakes.

The Inner Voice

Never ignore your instincts and
trust your first judgment.
We have been blessed with a
spirit that already knows,
Stay close and listen to that inner voice
because it will save you from troubles.
Have a positive mindset but be wise.
Pay attention to your dreams and
learn how to interpret them.
Speak good things and try to fill your mind
with good things through what you choose
to hear, see or hang around with.
Choose your friends wisely and
recognize the gifts they bring,
Invest in good friendships those who add
positivity and productivity to your life.
Enjoy being a female and having
female friends because we have been
blessed with extra intelligence.
Keep moving forward no matter
how many times you fall or fail.
Learn from your mistakes and the
mistakes of others and move on.

Accept what is and don't try to figure
out why, it will drive you crazy, unless
God chooses to reveal it to you.
Love with all your heart soul and mind. Love
God through loving and helping others.

Roller Coaster Love

Our love is like a rollercoaster baby.
Too many ups and downs and round
and round, here we go again.
Make ups to break ups you know it's
gotta stop, right here right now.
And I don't care how.
Just as long as we're not in the same house.
You either keep me or let me go
And if I'm for keeps just let me know.
I wanna be with you but I can't
If one day your my enemy then my man.
You gotta be faithful, honest and true
Coz I'm sick and tired of seeing
two sides to you.
We gotta keep it moving, moving, moving on x3
Stop being unpredictable baby
When I think it's all good like that.
You change your mood and we go right back,
To square one...I'm leaving you again.
Two days later I'll be back with you again.
I can't pretend, ain't no denying
You make me laugh and then I'll be crying.

And that's not right!
For my tears to drown my pillows at night
I can't keep up this fight.
Either we stay together or it's over
Coz the next man says move over.
We gotta keep it moving, moving, moving on x3

Pieces of Me

Pieces of me will always be with ya,
Pieces of me can paint a picture.
A picture, a painting of my soul
That tells a story worth more than gold.
Anytime I don't know the answer
I search deep within
To retrieve the pearls of wisdom within.
Thinking outside the box, but the box is not
Something outside of ourselves, or sitting
on top of a shelf collecting dust.
It's the trust that we have in our own instinct
Learning to go with what we first think
Not allowing others to sink our ship of treasures
Through discouragement and the belief
that you will never achieve your goal.
Tell them no.
And press on through the winds of opposition
Like a tree stand firm in your position
And when the wind blows against you listen.
To that inner voice saying 'stay on the mission'.
Just stick to your assignment
You shall bear fruit it just isn't time yet.

Beauty Is In The Eye of The Beholder

Beauty is in the eye of the beholder
Vision is subjective.
We all see things in a different way
I guess that was the objective.
We all have a purpose on the earth
No man can know it all.
Teamwork makes the dream work
No matter how great or small.
What do you have to contribute?
What are you known for?
Your purpose is significant for
all to share and adore.
Keep working at your craft
Whether it is serving, loving or giving.
Never think your gift is too small
All seeds are small in the beginning.

A Prayer of Gratitude

Have an attitude of gratitude. Each and everyday count your blessings and you will receive more of what you are thankful for. Like children don't hold grudges but move on from hurts and anguish as it is only detrimental to you. Forgive quickly as it is healing for your soul. Enjoy each moment of everyday to the fullest. Love with all your heart no matter how many times it's been broken. Failures have the purpose of sharpening your character and allowing you to appreciate the goal, once you do achieve it. I failed my driving test and even crashed straight after passed but now I'm a very cautious driver. I failed at getting onto my teaching course and had a difficult time during my PGCE and teaching days, but I have learnt to refine my teaching skills and feel that I am a better teacher because of it. My point is that even through failure there is always something to learn. You will realize it in hindsight but nevertheless, it was good for me to be afflicted. Thank you Father for everything!

Life

Life is like a box of chocolates you
never know what you gon' get.
Life is like is like an hour glass
so don't live with regrets.
Life is an experience a time to learn and grow.
Life is a circle you reap what you sow.
Life is good so enjoy the fruits of your labor
Life is beautiful each moment you should savor.
Life is a surprise it gives and it takes.
Life is a teacher so learn from your mistakes.
Life is like a game of chess,
plan your next move.
Life is balanced sometimes you win or lose.
Life is a race but it's not for the swift.
Life is a miracle it truly is a gift.

What Is Your Purpose?

Find your purpose, live your dream
Contribute to the earth, bear fruit, plant seed
Give freely and with joy because that is love
Be a wise as a serpent but as
harmless as a dove
Have discipline at least to control yourself
Eat the right food to maintain your health
Read books for pleasure and
to expand your mind
Exercise the body then relax and unwind
Work hard, play hard that is the key
Balance is essential for every part of me.

My Goal

My goal is to become what God wants me to be.
To enjoy life to the fullest, with
my loved ones around me.
To be creative through words, actions
and speech. To be a pioneer and be a
leader. To spark ideas and run with those
who know the way, those that have been
before me and my contemporaries.
I am so grateful for life and everything in
it. Including the hardships as that is what
defines my character. My purpose is to give
love and serve on the earth no matter how
hard it gets. Life is good, I cannot complain,
through it all including the hardships and pain
my God has explained the reasons I must go
through. Thank you Father for everything!

Clean Slate

This is a new chapter and a new day
What will you achieve?
What will you dream or believe?
What will you hope? If you dare to hope again.
What will you learn? Or is this the end?
I hope not...somewhere deep down in your well
is a fresh water supply. There is a light at the
end of the tunnel, you just have to go through.
Draw it out and produce something new,
something you are proud of if you
haven't done so already.
Just the voice of someone who
is running the race...

Printed in the United States
By Bookmasters